COAL MOUNTAIN ELEMENTARY

COAL
MOUNTAIN
ELEMENTARY

MARK NOWAK

WITH PHOTOGRAPHS
BY IAN TEH
AND MARK NOWAK

COFFEE HOUSE PRESS
MINNEAPOLIS :: 2009

COFFEE HOUSE PRESS books are available to the trade through our primary distributor, Consortium Book Sales & Distribution, www.cbsd.com or (800) 283-3572. For personal orders, catalogs, or other information, write to: info@coffeehousepress.org.

Coffee House Press is a nonprofit literary publishing house. Support from private foundations, corporate giving programs, government programs, and generous individuals helps make the publication of our books possible. We gratefully acknowledge their support in detail in the back of this book.

LIBRARY OF CONGRESS CATALOGING-IN-PUBLICATION DATA
Nowak, Mark, 1964–
Coal mountain elementary : new and selected poems / by Mark Nowak.
p. cm.
ISBN 978-1-56689-228-5 (alk. paper)
1. Coal miners—Poetry. 2. Working class—Poetry. I. Title.
PS3614.096C63 2009
811'.6—DC22
2008052608

FIRST EDITION
3 5 7 9 8 6 4
Printed in the United States

Special thanks to the editors and staff at the following journals who first published excerpts from this book: *American Letters & Commentary* #19 (2008), *Bombay Gin* 34:1 (2007), *NOR: New Ohio Review* no. 3 (2008), and *West Coast Line* 57 (2008).

Special thanks also to Professors Peter Okun, Bill King, and April Daras at Davis & Elkins College who first brought me to Elkins, West Virginia, for D&E's "Writers Week" just a few weeks after incidents documented in this book and who brought me back for the premiere of an excerpt of this text, under the title *Sago,* at D&E's Boilerhouse Theater on March 23, 2007 (funded in part by a grant from the West Virginia Humanities Council). It should go without saying that this project would have been impossible without their friendship, support, and artistic vision.

for Lisa, the adjectives

& for everyone mining beneath our feet, across the globe,
this morning and tomorrow

TABLE OF ILLUSTRATIONS

CONTENTS

FIRST LESSON

Coal Flowers: A Historic Craft

OVERVIEW: Students observe the process of crystallization in the making of coal flowers, a historic craft among coal mining families.

A 40-year-old woman has been waiting in a small room about 50 metres from the mouth of the Sunjiawan colliery since Monday afternoon's underground explosion. Compared to other distraught relatives clustered in the meeting room, where miners usually gather before descending into "the hole," the 40-year-old looked rather calm, a witness said. As a miner's wife, she said she had prepared herself for this day, but still it came too soon. "We didn't have the traditional new year lunch together because he had to work," she said. "His only day off for the whole year was [Lunar] New Year's Eve. We cooked dumplings. It was a good time." Her husband had been eager to get back to the hole, his wife said, "because he could get double pay on New Year's Day." She said she was not particularly sad but feared the scene when the dead would be brought to the surface and laid out in cold rows on the ground, awaiting identification. "I have no language for my feelings," she said. "And there's no way anybody else can understand it."

And that morning I just — I did actually notice though and I made the comment of an old wive's tale, you know, what does this mean, this lightning and thunder in January because where I'm from there's always a — you know, the frogs in certain part of the year and things like that. But I went to the door and opened the door because it was lightning and thunder carrying on so bad and it was so warm for the second day of January. You know, I asked two or three people, you know, what could this mean, you know. I mean, there's got to be a tale of some sort, you know.

OBJECTIVES:

Students will:

1. re-create the historic process of making coal flowers,

An explosion at a coal mine in north-eastern China has killed more than 200 miners, the worst known disaster to hit the country's accident-plagued industry in half a century. State media said yesterday 203 miners had died in the blast at Sunjiawan pit in Liaoning province on Monday. A further 22 were injured and rescuers were labouring to reach 13 still trapped. It comes after a series of accidents last year that included an explosion in northern Shaanxi province that killed 166 miners in November and a blast in central Henan that left 148 dead in October. During a visit to the site of the Shaanxi disaster last month, Wen Jiabao, Chinese premier, described the tragedy as a "lesson paid for in blood" and called for greater attention to safety to avoid any repeat. Mr. Wen's lunar new year's day pit visit, during which he ate lunch with miners underground, reflected efforts by China's leadership to stress its commitment to the welfare of ordinary workers and citizens. State media photographs from Sunjiawan yesterday showed miners clustered under billboards with government-promoted slogans such as: "Safety is the Sky and Quality is the Earth" and "Your Loved Ones Yearn for Your Safe Return."

Like on arrival at the mine, I went into the bathhouse and changed out of my street clothes into my mining clothes, put on, you know, my hard hat and my mining belt and boots, my rental uniform. And you know, we kind of sat around, joked with everybody, told stories and whatnot until it was time to go down over the hill. Proceeded over to the lamphouse, got my earplugs, cleaned my safety glasses, checked my light out and made sure it was working, put it on. You went down over to — into the pit.

OBJECTIVES (cont.):

2. make observations
   about the crystallization process
   that occurs during this craft, and

3. understand the role
   that the practice of making
   coal flowers played
   in coal mining families.

I always just talked to the guys until it was time to go in. We went over the hill and Two Left left, and we had to change a mantrip so we were behind them. And I got to my head about — Four Head about probably 6:15, something like that. When I got there, I fueled my duster up, got it going. Ate a cake and drank a milk and just walked out on my belt line and that's when it happened.

Xiao Wei has stopped tearing pages from the calendar hung on her broken wardrobe since Monday, when her father did not return from work. The teenager's 37-year-old father was one of the 244 miners who went underground on Monday at the Sunjiawan colliery in the Liaoning province city of Fuxin. As of yesterday, 210 of the 244 were reported dead from a gas explosion and rescuers were still searching for five missing miners. For Xiao Wei and her mother, Li Li, who declined to use their real names for fear of getting into trouble with authorities, the past two days have been hell, without word of whether the father and husband was alive or dead. Although relatives kept close, Ms. Li wept uncontrollably and fell into moments of exhaustion waiting for news of her husband. She knows in her heart that he is probably dead. "I am not prepared at all. He just left suddenly . . . and this is still the Lunar New Year," Ms. Li almost yelled through the tears. Xiao Wei, 14, held her mother's hands and sobbed quietly. "They forced him to leave 300 yuan as a deposit so that if he did not return to work after the Lunar New Year, they would deduct 100 yuan each day," Xiao Wei said. "Now what will happen to us, we have to look after old people and kids." Ms. Li said her husband started work as a coal miner two years ago because he wanted to earn more to pay their rent and Xiao Wei's tuition fees. "He used to be a security guard but he only earned 400 yuan [a month]. Our daughter is growing up now and will soon go to secondary school," she said. "That is why he began working as a miner and could earn about 1,000 yuan a month." Ms. Li's sister said: "Otherwise, who would take such a job? It is a job for living people working in hell."

NATIONAL
STANDARDS:
National

Science
Education
Standards:

Science
as Inquiry,
K–4, 5–8;

Abilities
necessary
to do scientific

inquiry;
Physical
Science, 5–8;

Properties of
matter
and

changes in
properties of
matter.

So I looked up at the clock, you know. And the clock's right there where you go out the door, and it was lightning real hard, thundering. And I opened the door and just raining to beat the band, you know. And I shut the door, and went that crack of thunder, my boss, Skip, or — James Scott's his name. He looked at me and George and he said that felt like an explosion. That's exactly what he said.

Open trucks filled with coffins made their way from mine to morgue through the streets of Fuxin, the freezing air thick with coal dust and the smoke from paper money burned in offering. Throughout the day, convoys of buses carried mourners bundled against the cold into a cemetery sealed off by security. Zhang Weiguo, a miner for more than 30 years, was the first to be cremated. "I touched his forehead, checked his teeth, then took off his shoes and looked at his toes . . . it is him but he is dead," his widow was quoted as saying.

Well, I felt this — we was setting there getting ready to go around the turn. I felt this kind of —. I didn't hear anything but a little bump, like a thump. And all this stuff started blowing down on us, coal dust, soot, ash, mud. It was just like volcano stuff, you know, it was just like being in a volcano. And I thought we was getting covered up with a roof fall at first. I said, oh, no, I'm going to get covered up in a mantrip, buried alive here.

TIME

NEEDED:

Two class

periods.

Zhou Liyuan, vice general-secretary of the Liaoning Provincial government, said at a press conference that the compensation work for the victims' families is well arranged and going on smoothly. He said 208 of the 214 bodies were claimed and 194 bodies were cremated. Family members of the 203 victims signed compensation contracts, and 146 families have received compensation money.

MATERIALS:

Shallow glass bowls

(one for each team of students),

Coal

(several lumps per work team),

Twigs

and/or toothpicks,

Small pieces of cloth,

paper,

or string,

Paper towels,

Glue,

Mixing bowls or cups,

I'll tell you just exactly like I told the senators and I told my son. If I put you in the bed of a pickup truck and I put that truck on the interstate, just everything that truck had in it, you couldn't get nothing more out of it, and then some way or another to fix it up so that somebody could get in front and throw sand, gravel, rock, blocks, mud, any and everything they could throw as hard as they could throw it in your face, that's close. That may be just a hair less, but it's close, for 10 — I said 8 to 10 to 12 seconds, some of them said it's 30 to 40, but —. And then it cut off, it — when it stopped, it stopped. There wasn't no gradual going down or nothing. It was one second, me and you are talking, the next second it's hitting you for everything it's worth, and then it's over with.

The death toll from a weekend gas blast that ripped through two coal mines in the north rose to 60 yesterday as rescue efforts to find nine more miners continued. The explosion occurred at the Xishui mine in Shuozhou city, Shanxi province, at noon on Saturday. The blast was so powerful that it blew through a safety partition wall and into the adjacent Kangjiayao mine. A total of 71 people were working in both mines at the time, CCTV reported. One of the 22 men working at the Kangjiayao mine was rescued soon after the blast and another made it to the surface by himself. The rest are either dead or missing. The ventilation systems in the two mines were working by yesterday morning, after overnight efforts by six teams hailed by Xinhua as the "most excellent rescue forces" ever mobilised in the province. Miner Luo Yuanbing, who said he counted himself lucky not to have been working in the mines on Saturday, said the blast was so strong it shattered windows in houses more than 100 metres away. "I was having my lunch and then the explosion came," he told Xinhua. "I said to myself: something terrible must have happened in the mines."

MATERIALS (cont.):

6 tbsp salt per work team,

6 tbsp laundry bluing per work team,

6 tbsp water per work team,

1 tbsp ammonia per work team,

Food coloring,

Thermometer

to measure air temperature,

Coal Flowers Worksheet

for each team.

Now, I lost everything exactly at 6:31. That's what the computer time was telling me. Like I said, I'll never forget it, because the Second Left section belt, the CO right there at the tailpiece, the CO midways at the belt and the alarm at the tail turned gray. Five belt went to power loss. Six belt went black, it went gray. It was like it didn't exist.

Dai Longcao said she had not been able to eat since the Sanhuiyi Coal Mine was ripped apart by a massive blast on Tuesday. "I held my children's hands and walked three hours along the mountain path to the coal mine," said the 42-year-old woman. "I took off immediately after I heard the news, and didn't even get a minute to let my parents know what happened." As her husband's meagre salary provides for the whole family, the housewife said she feared for the future of her son and daughter. Her fears were shared by a pair of sisters whose spouses were also their families' only breadwinners. Xia Xingrong and Xia Xingbi have their fingers crossed for their missing husbands. "If anything happened we'd be helpless," they said.

MATERIALS (cont.):

If the grocery
or hardware store
does not carry laundry bluing,
check with a pharmacy.
It can also be ordered
through many women's magazines
or purchased over the Internet
at www.mrsstewart.com.

I threw the phone down because lightning ran in on the phone. I told Jeff — I picked back up the phone and said, Jeff, there's something wrong. I have immediately lost all communications. I said, the belts is going down. As soon as it happened, I said I lost all the belts and everything. It popped the phone. Just like a pop on the phone itself. Just like noise, like electric. I threw down the phone and looked — I mean, a split-second — when I was talking to Jeff, I just threw it down. It hurt my ear. I picked up the phone and told Jeff that we lost the belts. Second Left is showing me just dead.

The death toll of a coal mine explosion last Thursday night in northwest China's Shaanxi Province rose to 21 as another miner died in hospital Monday evening, rescuers said on Tuesday. Zhang Zhifeng, a miner injured in the explosion, was rescued Saturday morning at Shangyukou Colliery, a private coal mine in Hancheng city. With serious burns and respiratory tract hurts, however, Zhang had been in a coma since being sent to hospital and died on Monday evening as all rescue efforts failed.

DISCUSSION QUESTIONS:

What do you know about crystals?

Where have you seen them?

How are they formed?

Have you ever heard of "coal flowers"?

If so, do you know when and how they were made?

Relatives of over 50 miners were last night hoping their loved ones had survived an underground blast at a coal mine in Chengde in North China's Hebei Province. Fifty one miners are believed to be trapped after the explosion at Nuan'erhe Coal Mine in the early hours of yesterday morning. It is unclear whether the trapped men are alive. Relatives of those trapped are keeping an emotional vigil at the colliery. "It's not clear whether they are alive or not," the State Administration of Work Safety's press official said.

I said, I'm going to stay in here and see what I can do because I got a brother up here. And I know — you know what I mean, I'm knowing that they're still trapped up there somehow, someways. And my men begs me to go with them, but I said, no, you all go. I said, I got to go see if there's anything I can do.

PROCEDURE:

1. Begin by explaining
   to students
   that the making of coal flowers
   is a historic craft that was practiced
   by coal mining families
   in the late 1800s and early 1900s.
   When mining families had
   little money
   to buy decorations
   or purchase toys,
   they used
   common household products
   and coal to make
   beautiful crystal flowers.
   It was entertaining to watch
   the crystal flowers grow,
   because the changes took place
   in a relatively short period of time.
   Coal flowers were sometimes used
   as Christmas decorations
   because they resemble
   snowflakes.

Rescuers said by Monday they had discovered 45 bodies at the site of a coal mine blast that occurred last Thursday in Chengde, north China's Hebei Province. Only one miner was rescued from the explosion scene. Another five miners remain missing. Sun Jisheng is the only one of the trapped miners who has been rescued. The former safety inspector, who was in a coma when he was brought to the ground on Saturday, woke up earlier Sunday but lost memory due to cerebral hypoxia for a long period of time, said doctors with the No. 266 Hospital of the PLA (People's Liberation Army) based in Chengde.

I had a little rough time, especially — well, stumbling around because I have an artificial leg and it's hard to walk on rough surface. The section foreman said I'm going back after my brother. So we told him he couldn't do that. So I said, well, what about my brother-in-law, so I broke out in tears then. And he said, well, I'm going to try to go find them.

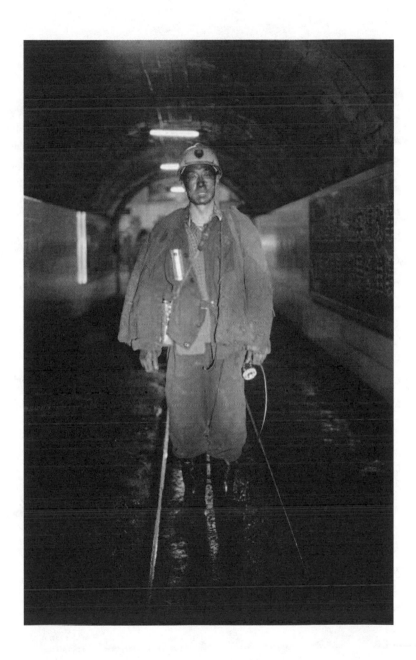

Living in a row of one-storey tiled houses with three kids, 40-year-old Cai Zhuhua has been struggling with life since her husband died in a mine tragedy that claimed 20 miners at the end of 2001. A 14-inch black-and-white TV and a rusty refrigerator are the most expensive items in her family's shabby two-room apartment. "Time has not dimmed the pain of losing my husband, and it never will," says Cai, who says that almost every morning at five, her husband rose to leave on an early shift after caressing her and the children and bidding them goodbye before closing the door. Cai is illiterate and now works as a part-time cleaner at the husband's Jianxin Coal Mine and says it has become increasingly hard to make ends meet as the kids get bigger. "High costs for education have hit us hard," says Cai, whose face shows anxiety and distress. With a total income of less than 700 yuan (US$87) per month, Cai had to make her eldest daughter drop out of high school last year to earn money for her younger sister and brother. The daughter has been persuaded by friends to go to work in Mianyang of Sichuan Province in Southwest China but has not been able to find a job there. "My sister's lesson has shown us how difficult it is to find a job and I should be well prepared," says Cai's second daughter Li Ying, 17, who has been burning the midnight oil to prepare for the coming college entrance examinations. Still sharing a room with her 16-year-old brother Li Hong, she is confident that she will pass the examination next month and hopes to study journalism at a university. "My dad didn't live a single day of a happy life, but I will try hard to earn a happy life for my mother," said Li Ying.

PROCEDURE (cont.):

2. In this activity,
   students will make
   their own coal flowers.
   Explain that the coal
   actually plays no chemical role
   in the creation of the crystals
   and is no more
   critical an ingredient
   than the toothpicks used.
   In addition,
   students will use
   food coloring to enhance
   the beauty of their coal flowers,
   although original coal flowers
   were made without
   this additive.

That's all I ever knowed him by is Doc. He's a little bit shorter than me. And I told him, I knowed he wore glasses like I did. I said, reach up and wipe off your glasses and wipe off the top of your hat — light so you can see. There's dust on it. And he said something else. And I said, well, I said, let's go. I said, we'll just ease down out of here nice and slow. I said, there's no great big hurry right now. We're all right. And he said, well, don't leave me. And I said, I'm not going nowhere. I'm going to be right here with you, come on, and I started backing up real easy. I had my dinner bucket and my rescuer. The reason I grabbed my dinner bucket, because I had the idea that we was going to walk out of there and somebody was going to need a drink of water. One other boy grabbed his water jug. And I eased Doc down around the side of the mantrip, and I told him when he got in to where his feet was inside that track, I said, you go down the track. Don't get out of the track, and I'm going to be right here with you.

Owners of a coal mine in Shanxi played down the death toll from an explosion two weeks ago by hiding or sending to neighbouring Inner Mongolia at least 17 bodies. The cover-up was revealed yesterday by the State Administration for Work Safety on its website. Rescuers found 19 bodies in the Jiajiapu mine in Ningwu county following a blast on July 2. But they could not determine exactly how many died. Authorities discovered after an investigation that the bodies of seven miners had been stored at a hospital. Another three were taken to a crematorium 150 km away in Ulanqab and seven more to Fengzhen, both in Inner Mongolia.

Well, I do remember the dispatcher saying we had an explosion. He repeated that out loud to himself and his face — his facial expression, he was real nervous and he was trying to figure out what was going on, what we needed to do and who we needed to call and —.

PROCEDURE (cont.):

3. Divide the class
    into manageable work teams
    of two to four students each.
    Give each group
    the necessary materials.
    Display the following procedures
    for each group to follow
    in making their coal flowers:

a. In the shallow bowl,
      place several small lumps of coal.

b. Arrange any combination
      of twigs, toothpicks, paper, cloth,
      or string with the coal.
      Use glue to hold
      the pieces to the coal if desired.

c. In a separate bowl or cup,
      mix the salt, laundry bluing,
      water, and ammonia.

d. Pour this mixture
      over the coal mound.

e. Sprinkle dots of food coloring
      over the mound.

Zhang Li, of the China Coal Industry Development Research Centre in Beijing, said most mainland miners lacked safety awareness and received little training. "Coal miners usually come from various provinces. Some of them are illiterate and most only have a primary education. They don't know how to protect themselves," Mr. Zhang said. "Many workers go down the mines the day they are recruited." He said miners today were generally one of the lower social classes in China. "They earn less than 1,000 yuan a month and many labour 10 hours a day every day." Wei Hailin, who has worked for more than 30 years at Pingxiang Coal Group in Jiangxi that has more than 3,000 small mines, said most miners were peasants desperate for work. "They know the danger but still want to be coal miners because they cannot make a living on the land."

PROCEDURE (cont.):

4. Distribute copies
   of the Coal Flowers Worksheet.
   Have students
   immediately complete
   the first three questions,
   documenting
   the air temperature
   according to the thermometer.

And Mr. Wilfong got off the Jeep there and asked the dispatcher if he had heard from the Two Left crew. They never had any communication with the Two Left crew. And we stopped at 25 block, at the phone again, and Dick Wilfong called the dispatcher and told him — I think his words were, we've got something bad wrong, call the state, the federal, get the mine rescue teams, get the emergency squad, get everybody out here.

The final death toll from Tuesday's coal mine gas blast in Northwest China's Shaanxi Province has been confirmed as 26, with the last two missing miners found dead on Wednesday night, local officials have announced. The accident happened on Tuesday afternoon, when 40 miners were working underground at the No. 5 Coal Mine in Jinsuoguan. Eleven of the miners escaped unharmed, three were injured and 26 were found dead deep in one of the tunnels, according to the Shaanxi Provincial Bureau of Coal Mine Production Safety Supervision. "The dead miners are all local farmers in Shaanxi and their family members and relatives have been in Tongchuan for the funeral proceedings. The local government may make proper arrangements for them and compensate the victims in accordance with the regulations," said Yang Jianbo, an official with the Tongchuan city government.

PROCEDURE (cont.):

If possible, document
the crystal formation
on an hourly basis
(either on the worksheet
or in a science journal),
noting change in size, shape, and color
or color vibrancy of the crystals.
Complete the rest of the worksheet
once the flowers are fully formed,
which should take no more
than eight hours.

When he told me that there was a problem at the mine, I questioned him where was the superintendent. And he told me that he was underground. I said, well, where is the maintenance superintendent. He's underground. Well, where's the safety director. He is underground. And I proceeded to make phone calls that morning. I started with our company people, calling phones and leaving messages on answering machines. Then I tried to call the state office and there was no answer of course at the state office. That was approximately 7:50 — 7:40, I'm sorry. 7:40. I got Mark Wilfong and Brian Mills' phone numbers off the answering machine. I called Mark Wilfong's home phone number. I let it ring ten times and there was no answer. I called Brian Mills' that was on the answering machine and got a message that the number had been disconnected. My wife was there helping me and I'm asking her to look up phone numbers in the phonebook. I then called John Collins at home, left a message on his answering machine. I then tried to call — I made so many phone calls, I don't want to get them mixed up. I tried to call the mine rescue team numbers that were on the board and was not having any luck with that. I made a phone call to Jeff Rice's home. He was not there. I made a phone call to the mine rescue station. This was approximately eight o'clock, maybe five minutes after 8:00. Their answering machine had been turned off. There was no answering machine. It had been turned off. I called Kenny Tenny's home and left a message on his answering machine. Then I called the District III office in Morgantown, and I had to call it twice to get all the phone numbers and names that were listed on their answering machine. I then called Carlos Mosley's cell phone number, which was listed on their answering machine, and I left a message. I called Bill Ponceroff's cell phone, left a message. I called Kevin Stricklin's phone and I left a message. I then had my wife look up Jim Satterfield's phone number. I called it and it was a wrong number. There was two Jim Satterfields listed in the book.

ASSESSMENT:

Place the experiment
in its historical context
by discussing why
this activity might be
a natural one
for coal mining families
in the late 1800s
and early 1900s.

Well, a little bit of time went by, and they kept trying to get ahold of people, you know, to see what had happened. And I'm going to be real honest with you. I've been around mining all my life, and I'll tell you what, I was nervous, because I know — this is because I've been around, I know the worse that could happen. So I was nervous. I wanted to see what I could do to help or whatever.

The mayors of Xingning and Meizhou have been suspended from duty for alleged incompetence in supervising a colliery that flooded on Sunday, leaving 122 miners trapped underground and feared dead. By yesterday — three days after floodwaters filled the Daxing Colliery in Xingning's Huanghuai town — only one of the trapped miners' bodies had been recovered. At a meeting chaired by Premier Wen Jiabao yesterday, the State Council ordered the creation of an investigation team to look into the disaster. The council also said the rescue operation should continue as long as there was a glimmer of hope. The council decision came as the first miner's body was recovered from 240 metres underground and brought to the surface at 3:45 a.m. An officer, surnamed Ye, of the Huanghuai police station near the mine, said the body floated up as rescuers were checking the water level.

ASSESSMENT (cont.):

Either photograph
the crystals
or have the students
draw them and explain
in their own words
how they made
the flowers.
They should describe
the process
as well as the changes
they noticed over time.

After we were outside maybe — again, I'm guessing, 5, 10, 15 minutes, because as soon as I got outside, I called my wife. And I gave the phone to another boy and I said, as soon as you call your wife, you give it to another guy and have him call his wife. Get all of us get our families notified. Don't tell them what happened, just tell them, okay, we're outside, we got a problem, and let it go at that. Because I knowed — and again, from a little bit different experiences, but close to it, that when all this started, the phones was dead to us. We couldn't talk to our families. And I didn't want any of the families to find this out over the scanner. Unfortunately, it did. You don't hide nothing from people. How these people found it out, I don't know, but they did.

Xiao Ying, the wife of a trapped miner, told Xinhua that her husband should not have died. "It wasn't my husband's turn to go down the pit, but the boss said there were not enough people and forced him to work. Now he will never come back," she cried. Her husband, 30-year-old Chan Dongming, has also left behind five-year-old and four-month-old daughters. She said the workers did not want to go down the pit, but the owner ignored their concerns. "The boss said that they couldn't work in the day time, but night time was available," Mrs. Xiao said. Zhao Xianming and another miner surnamed Ke from Jiangxi backed the claims. They said they worked around the clock in two or three shifts each day until an accident in another pit on July 14 killed 16 miners. "We stopped for a short period after that, but started working secretly on the night of August 6," Mr. Zhao said.

We must have got outside about 7:30, before 7:30. Because my wife said I called her at 7:33 on the cell phone to tell her I didn't want her to see it on the news, you know. I told her what happened. I was okay, so she wouldn't see it on the news and go off the deep end.

EXTENSION:

To more thoroughly understand
the role that temperature plays
in the crystallization process,
repeat the experiment
under heat lamps
and in refrigeration.
Make sure to document
the air temperatures
and contrast
the timing of the process
at different temperatures,
as well as the color vibrancy
of the crystals.

I called my daughter and wife. I don't remember which one answered the phone. I believe it was my wife answered, yeah. And told her that the mine had blew up and her brother was still in there and told her to come on up to the mine.

On Monday, rescuers said heavy rains forced them to suspend their search for 122 miners missing since Aug. 7, when millions of gallons of water flooded the Daxing Colliery mine in southern Guangdong province, trapping the men about 1,400 feet below the surface. Relatives have been asked for DNA samples to help identify any bodies recovered after long exposure underwater. Relatives and friends of the trapped miners have descended on Xingning. Many are staying at the state-owned Forestry Building hotel. One of them, Zhong Wenfeng, came to comfort his girlfriend, Li Meili, who lives in Hunan province. Her father and two brothers were trapped in the mine and were still missing Monday. "The one sound we hear at the hotel is crying," Zhong said.

DIFFERENTIATION:

Challenge

higher-level students

to research

and report

on the actual

chemical

reactions that caused

the crystallization

on the coal.

Guangdong authorities yesterday officially abandoned efforts to find the bodies of miners trapped at the flooded Daxing Colliery in Meizhou. Zeng Haiying, spokesman for the Meizhou government, said all 123 miners were now considered dead. "We cannot officially declare them dead, but an official declaration will be made by the local court soon," he said.

SECOND LESSON

Cookie Mining

OVERVIEW: Students participate in a simulation of the mining process using chocolate chip cookies and toothpicks. The simulation helps to illustrate the costs associated with the mining of coal.

A mine owner and the local government department in Shaanxi Province in Northwest China are accused of bribing reporters and relatives of accident victims to conceal news of a fatal coal mine accident. The accident was caused by burning gas in Qinfenggou West Coal Mine in Huangling County early morning on Thursday. Six miners working underground were killed, the bureau learned from a report by an insider on Saturday. After the accident, He Mingshan, owner of the private coal mine, and the Huangling County Coal Industry Bureau allegedly tried to cover up the truth and tried to bribe local reporters who went to cover the event, sources said. "They tried to put some cartons of cigarettes and bottles of wine into my car," said Chen Youmo, a reporter from a local news organization. The mine's owner allegedly handed the relatives of the two dead miners 200,000 yuan (US$24,661) each as compensation and to keep quiet about the accident. "The mine's owner urged me and other relatives of the dead miners to go back home as soon as possible after receiving the money and told us not to tell the truth to anyone," said Liu Qinxiang, wife of Yuan Chaoyin who was killed in the accident.

That one fellow, I can't remember his name. We talked about him over and over. I know he continued to — he was on One Left crew. He came out and he sat in Dick's office. And every couple minutes, he kept yelling for Two Left, Two Left, Two Left. I don't know if that's important, but I know that the guy was back at the shower house this time, because there was just so much going on inside the lighthouse that I just left. And you could hear him hollering for them, just — for hours.

OBJECTIVES:

Students will:
1. participate in
   a simulated "mining"
   of chocolate chips
   from cookies,
   using play money
   to purchase
   the necessary property,
   tools, and labor;

A mine explosion left at least five miners dead in Xinjiang yesterday, one day after 34 workers were killed in a pit in Henan province. The accident came in the wake of a call from Premier Wen Jiabao for local governments to pay special attention to prevent industrial accidents. Yesterday's blast rocked the locally owned Yatuer Colliery in Baicheng county at about 10:45 a.m. Twenty-five workers were underground at the time of the blast. Only 11 escaped, while five bodies were recovered by rescue workers last night. It was the second serious industrial accident since the start of the week-long "golden week" holiday on Saturday. The accident alarmed the central government, but with a death toll of less than 30 it was only classified as a medium-sized industrial accident under new regulations issued in July and did not need to be reported to Beijing.

Then after that, we just walked around. I had a family member come and check on me. I walked over to the pit and just stared at the pit for a long time, just hoping to see them walk out.

Anxious relatives demanded to be allowed into a coal mine Monday after an explosion killed at least 138 miners and left 11 others missing, adding to a soaring death toll in China's mines despite a safety crackdown. The disaster came as the nearby city of Harbin was struggling to recover from a toxic spill in a river that forced the government to cut off water supplies for five days. Outside the Qitaihe mine in China's northeast, emergency vehicles with flashing red lights and black government sedans made their way up and down the narrow, two-lane road to the mine entrance. Security guards blocked the front gate as about a dozen people stood outside in freezing weather and fog. Four women argued with the guards, demanding to be let in to look for missing relatives. "Why won't you let us in?" one shouted. When the guards refused, the women shouted obscenities at the men.

OBJECTIVES (cont.):

2. understand
   the various costs
   associated with mining coal,
   including environmental remediation,
   as demonstrated in the simulation; and
3. calculate costs and profits
   from cookie mining
   and relate them to the mining industry.

I never looked at my watch. The only time my watch even came into play is I broke the band on it when I stuck it in my pocket.

NATIONAL
STANDARDS:
National

Council for
the Social Studies
Standards:

Production,
Distribution,
and Consumption;

Science,
Technology,
and Society.

National
Council
of Teachers

of Mathematics
Standards: Numbers
and Operations, 3–5.

And I just mingled around, waiting to see what was —. Waiting on the other crew to come out. I thought surely the other crew would be coming out right behind us. And that didn't happen.

Government television in Heilongjiang province, where Qitaihe is located, showed an injured miner, his face black with coal dust, being led from the mine and collapsing onto a stretcher. "We couldn't breathe," said one miner as he lay on a stretcher. Provincial Gov. Zhang Zuoji was shown visiting survivors in the hospital. Most wore oxygen masks and many lay in bed still in their work clothes, their faces caked with black grime. Zhang rushed to Qitaihe from Harbin, about 250 miles to the west, where he had just taken part in festivities marking the restoration of running water that was suspended after a spill of toxic benzene in the Songhua River. Following the latest blast, President Hu Jintao and Premier Wen Jiabao urged officials to curb the "possible occurrence of big safety accidents which claim huge casualties," the state newspaper China Daily said.

TIME

NEEDED:

One

to two

class

periods.

And then some of the family members was coming in. The dressing room was split, you know. It's got a wall, like, in the middle. You can dress on both sides. We was over on the one side and the family members come in there, we moved over in the other side, you know, out of their way. And there's a guy there, he asked us to step back with the family and have prayer. We stayed back there with the family and we had prayer with them. We stepped back over on the other side.

Officials at the mine refused to discuss the disaster, but video on China Central Television showed gaping holes in numerous places at the mine site where explosions had ripped through the earth. "It's all the management's fault," a woman surnamed Ge, whose nephew and brother-in-law were among the missing, said as she stood outside the gates of the mine. "They knew all along that there were safety problems but they wouldn't do anything about it." A dozen other relatives of the missing stood nearby in below-freezing temperatures, some crying or sobbing. Ambulances were seen rushing out of the mine gates.

MATERIALS:

Play Money,

Three different types

of commercially packaged

chocolate chip cookies,

Grid paper,

Pencils,

Flat toothpicks,

Round toothpicks,

Paper clips,

Cookie Mining Worksheet.

"I believe a miracle will occur," says 23-year-old miner Yang Dayong. But hope is dimming as the number of deaths climbs to 148 and the list of those unaccounted for dwindles to just 3. Xinhua reported that the mine's chief engineer told the investigators that the management discovered the colliery had been building up five days before the explosion. Accompanying his mother, whose eyes have no tears left to cry, Yang, like everyone in the community, knows how vulnerable a miner's life can be. Together with his mother and younger sister, Yang was preparing a late dinner on Sunday evening for his father. The 42-year-old was expected to climb out of the mine at 11:00 p.m. "A bang at around 9:40 p.m. shocked us," said Yang, who lives three minutes walk from the mine. He had been working the day shift on Sunday and had made his way above ground at 3:00 p.m. "I escaped the explosion by just a few hours." He said his father, uncles and brother-in-law were digging in the third mining zone, the most geographically complicated of the mine's 15 zones, where the rest of the missing workers worked before the explosion. "We are crying for the rescue team to reach them as soon as possible."

And we went down to the sawmill plant. We was in a room there. We stayed there for a little bit, and I believe it was the press, they had put them a place. We left there and we went to — over to the tipple, because they weren't there. And we stayed at the tipple. And they was coming by — like, when they found out something, they'd tell the family members, and they'd stop by and tell us and then go to the reporters. I stayed there, and I got home probably about 8:00 or 8:30 that night, cleaned up. Well, I half showered at the plant and you know, finished cleaning up at home. And it was on the news. I started watching the news, and I watched it until all I could.

DISCUSSION QUESTIONS:

What do you think are some of the costs associated with mining coal?

Lying on a bed in Qitaihe Coal Mine Bureau Hospital, 41-year-old gas monitor Kuang Pingqiu is still in shock. Kuang is not only a survivor, he is also a hero for bringing two fellow miners to safety. Dong Baoliang, 31 and 47-year-old Liang Qinbai, owe their lives to Kuang. "We didn't know each other before and even now, I've no idea what his name is," said Dong, who lay in the next bed to Kuang. Dong was cutting up blocks of coal, like a meat slicer, dumping the broken shreds onto a conveyor belt taking it to the surface. When the explosion happened, he was dumbstruck, his head swam as he fought his way through the network of tunnels. "I didn't know where to go and just staggered aimlessly. Several times, I tried to wake up some co-workers but failed," said Dong. He does not know what happened to the 21 men he was working with. He said he finally met Kuang in a tunnel which was relatively rich in oxygen." At that time, I really didn't know where to go to safety." After struggling in the tunnel for 12 hours, they reached a lift which took them to the surface. "You cannot imagine spending 12 hours in underground darkness surrounded by deadly gas," said Kuang. "I was confident that I could save myself and others," Kuang added. "I saw rescuers waiting in the elevator underground, they acted too slowly."

So whenever a decision was made to explore, when not to explore, when to advance, when to withdraw, those were decisions that were made by the group; is that right? *Yes.*

So it would be representatives of ICG, the State of West Virginia, Federal. And was there miners' representatives at that time? *No.*

Do you know what the term land reclamation means?

If not, what do you think it might mean with regard to coal mining?

Everything was the same color gray or black, whatever you want to call it, from the soot and the dust. So I was taking my time and I was walking up the track entry. Bailey's team was about two or three crosscuts ahead of me, waiting on me up at the track entry to change out the batteries. And I got about a block away from them when I saw what happened to be two feet. It was Mr. Helms laying on the left-hand rib. And I called up to Bailey's team and I said — I asked them if they saw what was back here, because I didn't know if it had been identified yet. And they pretty much told me that there was debris everywhere. And I said, no, we got a man laying back here. And Bailey's team come back, and it was at that time that we found Mr. Helms.

"If this kind of situation continues, sad stories will increase," said a local taxi driver. "The sadness not only haunts the city today, what has happened will continue to haunt us for years to come."

PROCEDURE:

1. Review the costs
associated with coal mining:
land acquisition, labor,
equipment, and reclamation.
Coal companies
are required by federal law
to return the land they mine
to its original, or an improved, condition.
This process, known as reclamation,
is a significant expense for the industry.

An explosion tore through a coal mine in northern China on Wednesday, leaving at least 62 workers dead and another 13 missing, the government said, the third disaster in recent weeks involving scores of miners. The latest accident highlights the Chinese government's continuing battle with mine safety despite repeated crackdowns and pledges by the leadership to improve conditions. Wednesday's explosion occurred at the privately run Liuguantun Colliery in Tangshan, a city in Hebei province, when 186 miners were underground, said an official with the Tangshan Coal Mine and Safety Bureau who would only give his surname Zhang. Zhang said 82 miners escaped on their own and 32 were rescued, but three of those later died. The bodies of 59 other miners had been recovered by early today and rescuers were searching for 13 people still trapped in the mine.

We called it outside the way that they were instructed to call it out, as an item. We found the first item. Basically they told us that they didn't want to move him at that time, to mark his location and to mark what we had. And that's what we did. We didn't move him at all. We marked the location where we found him, marked it on the — it was either on the rib or on the roof. I'm not sure exactly where we marked him. And we covered him with a piece of canvas. And I didn't get the briefing outside, so I don't know where the fresh air base was going originally. But I know because of the location of the body, that they decided to put the fresh air base over in the intake entry and move it so that people weren't going right past the body.

PROCEDURE (cont.):

2. Explain that
   the mining industry,
   like any other business,
   faces challenges
   to make itself
   profitable.
   To understand
   some of these challenges,
   students will attempt
   to conduct a profitable
   mining business
   in an experiment
   that requires them to mine
   the "coal" chips
   from chocolate chip cookies.

When we got back to the fresh air base, the backup team had performed a task that we were initially sent in to recover the first miner that they located. And he was on a stretcher that was loaded in another scoop in the intake, but he wasn't in a body bag. So our team took a bag over and prepared him to be brought out. Otherwise he was just covered up with a blanket. And it wasn't very — I don't want to paint a disparaging comment. It wasn't really a professional, I guess, way of bringing the gentleman out. He was strapped on this backboard with a blanket covering him up. So we took him off the backboard and put him in a body bag, put him back on the stretcher. And I said backboard, but I think it was a stretcher. Put him back on the scoop. And then we waited for further instructions from command.

A rescuer was quoted by Xinhua yesterday as saying the chances of finding more survivors in Liuguantun were slim because of the high concentration of gas after the underground explosion. "Technically speaking, survival is possible. But it's hard to say how big the chances are," a rescuer said. Xinhua said 188 miners had been underground last Wednesday at the time of the explosion, but national safety chief Li Yizhong publicly reprimanded mine staff for their failure to keep accurate records of who was at work at the time of the accident. "[I] have no confidence in you," Mr. Li was quoted as saying by China News Service when confronting the mine managers. "Your labour record is a mess." Family members and relatives of miners gathered outside the mine yesterday, desperate for news. "We don't know anything. The government and the mine have not told us anything. What can we do?" one woman said.

Liuguantun, an ordinary village in North China's Hebei Province, suddenly fell into the limelight and occupied the headlines of major Chinese media overnight. What made the tranquil village become famous is a colliery explosion, a fatal accident that killed at least 87 miners and caused 21 others to go missing on Wednesday, November 30. In the yard of the coal mine were dozens of police cars, funeral vehicles and ambulances parked side by side; scores of rescuers in yellow uniforms entered and exited from a pit that had swallowed dozens of lives. The explosion is believed to be the most serious accident in the mining history of Tangshan, a city rebuilt on the debris of a heavy earthquake 29 years ago. Moreover, it was the third major blast within two weeks in the nation. A November 27 explosion in the Dongfeng coal mine in Heilongjiang Province killed 171; and on December 2, 42 miners died when a mine flooded in Henan Province, reports said. Two days after the blast, people were beginning to believe that the surviving hope for the trapped ones was fading, despite the intensified rescue efforts. Choking gas had forced rescue teams to retreat from the mine several times to wait for repairs to its ventilation system, said officials in charge of the rescue. As the smoke clears, Tangshan is grappling with the blast's aftermath.

PROCEDURE (cont.):

3. Give each student
   $19 in play money,
   a sheet of grid paper,
   and a Cookie Mining Worksheet.
   Allow each student to purchase
   one "mining property" (a cookie)
   from three separate brands available.
   Montana costs $3,
   Pennsylvania costs $5,
   and Kentucky costs $7.
   Students may want
   to examine the cookies
   before deciding
   which one to purchase.

It was just an Excel spreadsheet with one that said — the column on the left was item and 1 through 12 — 1 through 13, actually, with the first item being the man that was found in the track heading. I forget his name now. And then, you know, the other column was the corresponding name of the individual. An item number, they just had more or less a code.

PROCEDURE (cont.):

4. Once all the students
   have purchased their property,
   have them measure it
   by placing it on the grid paper
   and tracing it.
   Then have them count
   the number of squares
   that fall inside the circle
   (partial squares count as full squares).
   Tell students to record this number
   on the Cookie Mining Worksheet
   under D. Reclamation.

Long Shengpei, 34, recalled the tragedy and called his survival a "lucky escape." "Dense smoke suddenly rushed into my face before I realized it was a gas explosion," Long said. Long, together with his six colleagues, tried with all of their strength to run for their lives. But the 300-metre lane before them seemed endless; three of Long's colleagues collapsed and later were found dead at the middle of the path. Long fell to the ground before he reached the entrance of No. 2 Lane. He then inhaled some oxygen by using a oxygen tank, and was carried to safety during the rescue, which began half an hour after the blast. Having worked in the coal mine for just two months, Long told reporters that the colliery did not train workers to use the breath machine at all. Long is from Guizhou Province and earned a salary of about 2,000 yuan (US$246.70) a month before the accident. When asked if he would still work as a miner after he recovered, he said he has no plans for the future. Some other injured miners also complained there were not enough oxygen tanks with them when they worked underground.

I heard the announcement, we have 12 — we have 12 alive. I looked amongst others in the room, waited on the reaction, because I didn't see anybody jump. And then I seen somebody pump their fist, then I realized that they had heard the same announcement that I did. I made a comment to someone the other day that I had touched the ceiling tiles when I jumped. I couldn't believe the announcement. I just thought it was fantastic. Then I took off running. I came in the back door, run out the side door towards the front of the mine office, screaming, yelling.

More than 150 Chinese coal miners were dead or missing yesterday following three separate accidents in seven days, prompting renewed calls for better safety in the nation's notoriously dangerous industry. The death toll from an explosion on Wednesday at the Liuguantun colliery in the northern province of Hebei rose from 74 to 87, as rescuers continued their search for at least 21 other miners still unaccounted for. In the central province of Henan, hopes were fading for 42 workers who have been trapped since the Sigou mine in Xin'an county flooded last Friday. "Water is still leaking into the mine . . . progress is going slowly," the State Administration for Work Safety said in a statement yesterday. There was no indication that rescuers had detected signs of life. In the third accident, six miners have been missing since the Changling coal mine in the northeast province of Jilin flooded early on Thursday, Xinhua news agency reported. The tragedies, which follow the deaths of 171 workers on Nov. 27 in an explosion at the state-run Dongfeng coal mine in the northeastern province of Heilongjiang, mark a terrible year-end for China's coal industry. The spate of accidents prompted some state-run papers to repeat calls for better safety and reforms. "It seems unlikely that hearts of gold could be installed in mine owners and managers," said China Daily in an editorial yesterday. More than 6,000 miners died in workplace accidents last year, according to government statistics. Labour rights groups say the figure could be as high as 20,000.

And I've only — at that time, I had only been drunk once in my life, but it was absolutely euphoric, the feeling there, because, you know, I had done the math a couple times before and I didn't expect to hear that, as far as, you know, one cubic air — one cubic yard per hour per man at rest. And I have to say even with the birth of my children, that was the happiest, most — best news I had ever heard in my life.

5. Have each student
   purchase "mining equipment"
   (flat and round toothpicks
   and paper clips).
   More than one
   piece of equipment
   may be purchased,
   but no tools may be shared
   among students.
   Sell a flat toothpick for $2,
   a round toothpick for $4,
   and a paper clip for $6.
   Sell replacement tools
   when necessary.

A colliery gas blast on Wednesday killed at least 23 miners and sickened 53 others in North China's Shanxi Province, local mine safety authorities said yesterday. Altogether 697 miners were working in the pit when the blast went off around 7:00 p.m. at Sihe Coal Mine under the State-owned Jincheng Mining Group, said an official with the provincial coal mine safety supervision bureau who declined to be named. "No more deaths will occur in the mine as the rest of the miners are all safe," Tai Jie, an employee of the general office of the mining group, told China Daily in a telephone interview yesterday. She was the only person on the managerial staff who could be reached to comment on the fates of the more than 600 miners. The tragedy happened on the fourth day of the Year of the Dog, according to the lunar calendar. Local sources told China Daily that most of the miners were from villages nearby who hoped to earn some extra money by working during the Spring Festival holiday.

PROCEDURE (cont.):

6. Explain
    that each minute
    of mining (labor)
    costs $1
    and that each
    chocolate chip
    mined from their property
    will result in a $2 profit.
    Broken chips
    may be combined
    to form a whole chip.
    Consumed chips
    will eat into profits!

It's not really a secret to me how the — it got conveyed over to the church. Everyone there had cell phones, and everyone — a lot of people there had family members at the — over at the church. And why would you not pick it up and call them, you know. I don't think a normal individual would even question that information. I never questioned it. I thought it was absolutely the best thing I'd ever heard. I never questioned that at all, but I can definitely see how it happened.

PROCEDURE (cont.):

7. Do not allow
   students to spend more
   than five minutes mining.
   If they spend less time,
   their labor cost will be lower.
   Have them record
   their mining time
   and labor cost
   under C.
   Mining/excavation costs
   on the Cookie Mining Worksheet.

Six miners died in a coal mine gas surge in Central China's Hunan Province over the weekend. Twelve miners still missing in the accident are feared to have suffocated to death. A local official said yesterday that the missing workers were unlikely to have survived despite the ongoing rescue efforts which have been going on round the clock. The methane gas surge happened at 5:00 p.m. on Saturday in Dayuan Coal Mine of the province's Longhui County when 24 miners were working underground. Six miners were saved. "The amount of gas is too much and those missing miners were probably suffocated to death," the head of the county's coal industry bureau, surnamed Huang, told China Daily. "There is no hope of survival."

And we got up to — I think it was the very last crosscut in the track, on the left side there was a curtain that was — it was up. It was nicely hung, I mean, like sealed. And we all stopped and looked and thought maybe that might be a barricade. You know, we just looked at it. So we went on up in and circled back around, and that's when we was in the last open and that's when we heard the noises that Randy McCloy was making. So myself and a State inspector went one way and the federal inspector, Ron, and Mike Clark and Jim Smith, which them two are off of McElroy's team, they went back around to maybe see if that was a barricade. But when I went through the curtain — actually, two curtains, one across the last open, then one diagonal, they were all there in the last — Number Three entry. I proceeded up — I mean, it was obvious who was making the noise, and I went directly to him and proceeded trying to help him. As the other team members came in and the State and the federal inspectors come in, they proceeded with the rest of them, checking pulse, checking everything. And as you all know, there was only one that —. So he was in a sitting up position, and I was trying to get his lips pried open to try to get air to him, and I couldn't get him.

PROCEDURE (cont.):

8. After everyone
   is finished mining,
   have students
   restore their property
   to its original condition,
   within the drawn circle
   on the grid paper.
   This "reclamation"
   should also be timed
   (no more than three minutes)
   and students may only use
   their tools, not fingers.
   After time is up,
   collect additional
   reclamation costs
   ($1) for each square covered
   outside the original outline.
   Disburse profits
   for chips mined.
   Have students use
   the Cookie Mining Worksheet
   to calculate
   their profit
   or loss.

So we got halfway down there, and Jim — I hear Jim yelling, they're here, they're over here. Get over here, I found them. So I take off on a dead run heading that way. And went on in there, through a curtain there just hanging there and went on in, and there they were, all — all — Jim's working on McCloy, because he's alive, you know, he's — and I go directly to the opposite side of him and start checking for pulse and — you know, any breathing on the guys on the right-hand rib. So I'm working my way down checking each one of these guys to make sure, you know — to see if they were alive, you know. Checking for a pulse, checking for breathing. And I get all the way down to the last guy and then Jim yells come over here and help me, I need some help. So I come over there to help him, and McCloy is still in a slouched position breathing really — I mean, his breathing was real low. But he was making a noise while he was breathing. And that's the noise we heard. You know, we heard a noise, and that's what it was.

Thirty-seven miners were killed in three coal mine gas explosions in the past two days, Xinhua and the national safety watchdog said yesterday. Two blasts occurred yesterday, one in Rongsheng Coal Mine of North China's Inner Mongolia Autonomous Region and the other in Taihe Mine in Qitaihe of Northeast China's Heilongjiang Province. The Inner Mongolia accident occurred at 4:00 a.m. yesterday when 34 workers were underground, said the State Administration of Work Safety (SAWS) on its website. Twelve miners have been pulled to safety, said an official with the Inner Mongolia Regional Bureau of Coal Mine Safety. But 17 miners were confirmed dead, and five were still missing, Xinhua reported last night. The Qitaihe blast occurred at 12:40 p.m. when 16 miners were working underground. Nine were killed and 7 rescued. In an earlier accident on Sunday in Central China, all 11 workers were killed after being trapped underground by an explosion that caused a cave-in at Gaoping Colliery in Hunan's Yongxing County, said a source from the provincial coal mine work safety bureau. Due to the high density of gas underground, rescuers could not enter the mine to search for the trapped, reports said.

ASSESSMENT:

Allow students to share their experiences with the class.

Was making a profit easier or harder than they expected?

How accurate is this simulation in illustrating the challenges of making money in the mining industry?

What costs or possibilities for profits were not included in this exercise?

So we were — and I don't know who all did it, but I know I did. I went to at least four or five of them trying to holler at them, tell them to wake up. I even put my hands on them, shaking them. Some of them I did not do that way. I remember that they took time to place curtain on the mine floor for them to sit on, that they had fixed theirselves — what we coal miners a bed to sit on. You know, coal miners just don't sit on the mine floor, they always lay something out. And that's one of the things that stuck out in my mind is, they had done that.

Unlike ordinary workplace accidents, four women employees were found among the victims of the fatal gas explosion at Dongtang Coal Mine in Maoyi Township in Hunan's Lengshuijiang, reported Xinhua. Five miners, including two further females, managed to escape the accident. The missing miners were unlikely to survive the tragedy as the ventilation system was ruined and tunnels blocked, while gas remained dense in the pit, rescuers said on Sunday. China's laws on labour and mine safety forbid women from working in shafts, said officials in charge of work safety. "According to the rules on the protection of female employees, the employment of women in pits is banned, alongside other physically-intensive or taboo labour," said an official surnamed Wang with the All-China Women's Federation yesterday. Wang told reporters that her federation, as well as other labour protection organizations, are trying to lobby the legislative bodies to amend the current laws and regulations to better protect the interests of women workers.

EXTENSION:

Encourage students
to design another
profit/loss simulation
for a different industry.
Remind them to think
of all the costs
related to the industry
and to try to create
an exercise that can be done
in a short period of time
by the rest of the class.
Have them prepare
a worksheet
for other students to complete
after participating in the simulation,
on which to calculate
their profit
or loss.

Electricity shortages slowed attempts to clear a flooded mine shaft Monday, and residents began to lose hope for 57 miners trapped for a fourth day in China's worst mining accident this year. Rescuers threaded hoses into the main shaft and carted steel pipes into a secondary entrance to the Xinjing mine in the dusty north China hill country, where poverty and China's massive appetite for energy are fueling risky and often deadly mining practices. With no ambulance or medical personnel on the site, it appeared rescuers were not expecting to find anyone alive from Thursday's accident. "We must go all out to rescue these men. But we also need to start preparing for the worst," Feng Lixiang, mayor of the nearby city of Datong, which administers the area, was quoted as saying in local newspapers. Shen Wenhui, a wife of one the missing miners, said she was "in despair" with no news of her husband.

I tried to check everybody's — I checked everybody's pulse. I felt for a pulse. And I think most of them had hemorrhaged, hemorrhaged out, and there was some physical evidence there that you could see. I mean, that I thought, you know, with the hemorrhaging, most of them had hemorrhaged and some of them, there was foam, a lot of foam, and a pulse. They were ice cold. And they appeared to be deceased.

Carbon monoxide poison is a natural-occurring gas. It happens in the atmosphere. We have levels of carbon monoxide in us all the time, because you can always test someone and find some portions of it. It's tasteless, odorless, so you don't know it's there. As it gradually builds, you have side effects, nausea, headache. Then at some point in time it gets to the point to where your respirations aren't effective, because carbon monoxide binds to your red blood cells more higher, more affinity — what we call affinity to your red blood cells than pure oxygen does. So when your red blood cells are transporting oxygen, they're not really transporting oxygen, they're transporting carbon monoxide, which cannot be used. And that cycle stays. And it's a very hard bond to break between the carbon monoxide and the red blood cells.

DIFFERENTIATION:

Working

in tandem

to complete

the profit/loss

worksheet

might be

helpful

for those

with math-related

learning

disabilities.

"How could you go so soon?" cried out Zhang Qiongying, clutching two photos of her 31-year-old husband, Tang Daoliang. She said she was sure he was dead. "If they'd started pumping it in the first 24 hours, there would have been a chance to save them," said Zhang, standing with her husband's sister outside the ramshackle concrete huts where miners live. She expressed anger that no one seemed to be taking care of the families or "taking responsibility" for the accident. The Xinjing Coal Mine flooded after miners dug beyond its assigned area and broke into an abandoned adjacent mine, the official Xinhua News Agency said. Mine manager Li Fuyuan and at least eight other officials have been detained for questioning, although the mine's owner fled, state media reported. Authorities accused them of dismissing reports of leaking water before the flood and trying to hide the number of missing miners. Miners who wouldn't give their names said accidents were frequent and complained that managers pressured them to dig faster or be fired.

The two older gentlemen. They were — this is my opinion. They were placed in a funeral home position, laid down, feet straight, nice and perfect, like some other of the guys put them over there and laid them out like that. My opinion, the rest of them were leaning up against a rib or laying in a fetal position, like they're sleeping and stuff, and these two were perfectly — like some religious person put them in that position. One was this way and one was this way.

Tang Xufang, wife of a missing miner, brought his clothes from a dormitory, piled them up and set them on fire, an old Chinese tradition that some believe allows their dead loved ones to use the articles in the afterlife. "Why did you abandon us so soon?" Tang yelled as she threw a pink suitcase on top of the fire. Tang said she last spoke with her husband, Xiao Guangshun, a day before the accident. He called her in their home province of Sichuan in China's southwest to say he had wired her $125. After the accident, Tang set off for the mine by train but couldn't get past police outside until Chinese reporters arrived hours later and demanded they open the gates.

THIRD LESSON

Coal Camps and Mining Towns

OVERVIEW: Students look at the history of the coal mining industry by researching coal mining towns built by mining companies. Students then write short stories that highlight the people who lived in coal communities, focusing on the relationship between the coal companies and the miners and their families.

When Mr. Wei was a young boy growing up here in the 1960s, he said, *Shangma Huangtou* was a village of about 500 people set up against the hills, with corn and soybean farms and a stream running through the middle of the village. "I remember you could drink from that stream," Mr. Wei said. Everyone here talks about the stream. "When I was young this stream was very clear," said Lin Youmao, the village's elected chief. "We could find fish and shrimp in this little river. And we could swim in it." In the early 1980s, however, when China was just waking from its long economic slumber, the village turned into a coal mining town after rich deposits were found in the area. Armand Hammer, the American industrialist and the founder of Occidental Petroleum, formed one of China's first joint ventures here in north China. In 1982, his company signed an agreement to create a huge open-pit coal mine in Shanxi Province, which had just been designated as the nation's new energy base. The mine was created about a mile east of the village. And when the new project broke ground, residents recall, Mr. Hammer flew in by private jet and Prime Minister Li Peng came for the ceremony. Years later, Mr. Hammer pulled out of the project, unhappy with its progress. But the An Tai Bao open-pit coal mine continued to grow, scooping up millions of tons of coal and piling mountains of coal waste next to the village.

So we drug him down and laid him out in a turned position, but we
had to move the guy — one of the guys that was next to him fell over
on his lap. He was — you know. And I checked him real quick to
make sure he wasn't — to see if he was alive, you know, but he was
fell over on his lap, and then you could see where he had bled a lot. I
mean, a good bit. Well, anyways, we moved him off, then we pulled
Randal down and got him laid down. And I'm rubbing his legs trying
to get circulation going, because it's cold, you know. And I'm rubbing,
trying to get circulation going in his legs, and just trying to get him
— and Jim says take over up here with this, and hold this in his
mouth, and you know, try to get him breathing. I said just wait, let
me get another one, I got another one I think, and we opened it up
and put it in his mouth, you know, just to make sure it was good, you
know. I believe I did. I can't really place whether I did or not, but I
think that we did. I'm not for sure. And I'm still trying — I'm rubbing
McCloy's head, you know, telling him it's going to be all right, we're
going to get you out of here, trying to get some you know — because
his eyes was open and he was looking, you know. You could tell he
was, you know, dazed or whatever. And we're — I'm trying —
rubbing his head. I'm concerned with him more or less anything else.
And you know, I'm trying to get him — you know, talking to him.
We're going to get you out of here, you know. You'll be all right. We're
going to get you out of here.

OBJECTIVES:

Students will:

1. gain an understanding
   of the historic role
   of the coal mining companies
   and the establishment
   of mining towns;

2. research and consider
   the relationships between
   miners, their families,
   and coal companies; and

3. create a fictional short story
   about a person or persons
   in a mining town.

The big gentleman that fell over on top of him — was on his chest, and he didn't — he wasn't taking as deep as breaths as the rest of the people. And I think that's probably — it kept him warm.

Some residents later talked about the village's founding myth, an old fable about how the beautiful village was founded in ancient times with a small lake in its center. But one day, according to the fable, a smart man from southern China came and stole the village frog, bringing ruin to Shangma Huangtou. "I don't believe this myth," Mr. Lin, the village chief, said. "I believe there's no water because of the coal mines. The earth is like the human body. And the water is like the blood in your veins. But now there's no water; no blood."

Jesus is Lord
The Way of the Cross Leads Home
Philippi Development Inc.
Sentinel Mine

But bringing him outside, I just didn't think that — I didn't think that this boy was going to make it, you know. After we put my machine on him, I felt like he was breathing a little bit quicker. You couldn't hear him gasp for breath, but his fingers was drawed up. And the track — and going outside, the track, if the mantrip would hit a kink or bump in the track, his eyelids was opening, and you'd see his eyes were rolled back in his head. You'd just see the whites of his eyes. And then going outside, I didn't think that this boy was going to make it.

Fifty-three people were confirmed dead from the colliery explosion in north China's Shanxi Province after the attempted rescue operation ended on Wednesday. The rescue operation headquarters said that 53 bodies had been retrieved, revising the figure that 59 miners, instead of 64 that was previously reported, were working underground when the blast hit the Linjiazhuang Coal Mine of Lingshi County, Jinzhong City, at about 4:40 p.m. Saturday. Six miners managed to escape and another one was rescued alive, the headquarters said, adding that another miner died from carbon monoxide poisoning while helping with the rescue operations.

NATIONAL STANDARDS:
National Council for
the Social Studies

Standards: Culture;
Time, Continuity,
and Change;

People,
Places, and
Environment.

National Council
of Teachers
of English

Standards:
Students
employ

a wide range of strategies
as they use different
writing elements

to communicate
with diverse audiences
for a variety of purposes.

I'm going to tell you, the only thing — carrying Mr. McCloy out, I was on the right-hand side in the back, close to his head. And what I was doing, and we all were doing it, we were talking to him all the way out. Hang in there, we're going to get you out. And I put myself, my eyes on his hand, and I noticed he had a wedding band on, and I'm thinking about this young man. And I watch his hand all the way out to see if he moved any, and that's what I did. I was watching to see if I could see any movements. But I did notice his wedding band on his hand. He never did move his hand that I could see.

Rescuers found the bodies of the last three missing miners in a coal mine collapse in northwest China's Xinjiang Uygur Autonomous Region Monday afternoon, bringing the death toll to 13. Another seriously injured miner was rescued Sunday and is being treated in hospital. Doctors said that he has not been out of danger yet.

TIME NEEDED:

Two class periods,

with time in between for research and writing.

MATERIALS:

Pen and paper,

A computer with Internet access.

DISCUSSION QUESTIONS:

Where and when did coal mining towns exist?

Who lived in them?

What role did coal mining play in the lives of those who lived in the towns?

Do you think these towns still exist?

We got him all the way to the neck and there was Kevin Strickland, a bunch of people standing there, and they're going, where's the rest of them. And that's just when we all — everybody carrying that stretcher just died. They just went —. That's when we first knew that miscommunications —. So I went over to the fresh air base and called outside and talked to Rick Marlow. And it was apparent that he didn't know. And finally, I had to tell him, you know. They wanted me to tell him items, item one, item two, you know. They didn't want no names coming over because they said people were eavesdropping and stuff like that. So I told him we had 11 items, and he said, what. I said, we got 11 items. And he said, forget the code. What do you mean? I said, there's 11 deceased people. And he was just — he was speechless. He couldn't —. They just asked where the rest of them were. I said, there is no others. And that was just when everybody just — the whole ye-hah stuff went sour. Yes, they didn't — no one knew — yeah. That's when the no survivors and all the survivors, that's when it — I can't describe what it was like.

PROCEDURE:

1. Begin
    by providing students
    with a brief history
    of coal mining towns.
    Explain that Pennsylvania
    was the largest coal mining state
    during the 19th and early 20th centuries,
    until West Virginia surpassed it in 1930.
    Wyoming has since surpassed
    West Virginia
    in mining productivity.
    In all three of these states,
    mining towns—
    known as coal patches
    or coal camps—
    were very common
    from the late 1800s
    to the early 1900s.

Twenty-nine people were confirmed dead and 19 injured in a coalmine gas explosion in Northwest China's Gansu Province, rescuers said yesterday. The explosion occurred at 12:16 p.m. yesterday at the Weijiadi mine belonging to Jingyuan Coal Industry Corporation in the city of Baiyin. A ventilation system was being checked when the blast occurred, said Wang Jun, general manager of the company. Workers above ground only realized an accident had occurred when a sudden blackout of gas monitoring and communication systems occurred at 1:36 p.m. They immediately started emergency procedures, Wang said. The 29 fatalities occurred at one level, where six miners were injured including one seriously. Thirty-six miners, including 13 injured, were rescued from other levels. All the injured are being treated at local hospitals. State-run Jingyuan Corp. has an annual output of 8 million tons of coal. It ranks 59th in the nation's top 100 coal producers according to Chinacoal Website, recording a turnover of 1.2 billion yuan (US$154 million) in 2005. In May, one of its mines was the site of a carbon monoxide poisoning accident that caused nine deaths.

But unfortunately, I said, you know, we got to confirm, you know, let's clarify it. And the room erupted, but we were still doing business. And I never seen so many old hairy guys cry in my life. But I was outside stretching my legs. I had sat in my chair so long that I was having trouble with my feet. And I don't know, it was sometime there after then, they called me back in, and they had used the code word, because we had told them not to say bodies over the phone. To use the word, you know, items. And that — you know, that confused us. And that's when, I don't know who it was, said they had — it was 12 dead and one alive, with his head that way. And that, that was the worst moment personally and professionally in my life.

PROCEDURE (cont.):

These communities
were created
by coal companies
so that workers could live
near the mines.
The coal companies
built and owned everything,
including schools,
churches, stores, theaters,
and residential structures.
Ask students to list
the pros and cons
of living in such towns.
Encourage students to think about
what other employment options existed
for some of these people,
who had limited education and skills;
what happened when
the coal mines closed down;
and how small communities
such as these
created a sense of family
among the residents.

Winter is a dangerous season for miners. Last week, at least 40 miners died or remain missing in the Xinjiang Uygur Autonomous Region, Jilin, Hebei and Guizhou Provinces, according to the website of the State Administration of Coal Mine Safety. "There is a much higher coal demand in the winter, which increases production," an official from the administration warned in a recent work meeting.

So I know it's somewhere — two and a half to three hour time frame went by, but from my perspective it all went by very quickly. It took an inordinate long time to get from the mine office over to the church due to the crowds. And then at that point we went to the church. And it was my understanding that the families had been notified already. It wasn't until I walked into the church and looked out on the crowd and saw all those smiling faces and all the happiness that I realized that they had not been notified. So the news was broken. Just the opposite of the jubilation that had occurred three hours earlier occurred in that church. It was just gut-wrenching.

PROCEDURE (cont.):

2. Divide the class into three groups.
    Assign each group one of the following
    coal mining states: Pennsylvania,
    West Virginia, or Wyoming.
    Tell students that they will be
    researching coal patches,
    or camps,
    in their assigned state.
    They are to find out as much as they can
    about the history of mining in that state,
    as well as the development
    (and demise, if relevant)
    of the mining communities.

We arranged for the three ambulances that was on site to go down close to the portal. There was some discussion that someone believed that there was reporters trying to get a shot of the bodies, you know, on the hills or a helicopter possibly, something like that, so we sort of — a couple of us got together and discussed how we could handle the bodies in a very respectful, you know, very delicate way when we had to bring them from the mantrips to the ambulances. So we kind of talked about that a little bit.

PROCEDURE (cont.):

In their research, students should seek
answers to the following questions:
What camps or patches existed in this state?
When were they built?
What coal companies owned the camps or patches?
What services in the camps were owned
and run by the coal companies?
What types of coal were mined?
Who (what ethnic groups)
populated the communities?
When did the communities flourish?
Did the mines stop producing? If so, when?
What does the community look like now?

3. Provide students with the following
    Internet links to begin their research.
    Encourage them to study
    the photos on these Web pages
    to get a feel for the appearance
    of each community
    before they begin
    gathering information.
    Give students ample time
    to conduct research
    and document their findings
    in their journal.

Seven people were killed in a colliery accident in Southwest China on Monday, bringing the death toll in coal mine tragedies to 85 over the past three days. Eleven workers who were sorting impurities from a coal heap were buried when the heap collapsed at 9:47 a.m. at the Shuicheng Coal Mine Group colliery, in mountainous Guizhou province. Seven workers died and four were rescued, said the work safety administration in Liupanshui city, where the group is located. The cause of the accident is being investigated.

.

PROCEDURE (cont.):

4. Once the groups
    have completed their research,
    have them work in pairs
    within their state groups
    to create short fictional stories
    about a historic coal patch or camp.
    Encourage them to write
    about realistic characters and settings.
    They should rely on their research data
    to provide accurate locations, time periods,
    and ethnicities for their characters.
    Allow them to be creative
    about the plot of their story,
    but tell them they must include
    some authentic details about
    the characters' work and home life.

We went through a — kind of a work in progress as to how we were going to do the body bags, how to be as courteous and caring with all the bodies as we could. A great deal of respect was shown by everybody in the handling of these folks. We tried as best we could to get folks in the bags, because again, it was a pretty gruesome job.

ASSESSMENT:

Have students
swap their stories
with pairs who researched
other states.
After sharing stories,
have them discuss
differences
in the mining history
and culture of the two states.

EXTENSION:

Research can also be conducted
on the coal camps of other mining states,
such as Illinois, Virginia, Ohio, and Kentucky.

China's work safety chief has lambasted municipal officials over Sunday's Changyuan coal mine gas blast in Yunnan, saying their defiance of provincial government orders to close illegal collieries was "vicious in nature." The emotional message from State Administration of Work Safety director Li Yizhong was televised nationally on Monday on China Central Television. Sunday's blast occurred at an illegal mine in Qujing. "What power do Qujing city government officials think they possess to defy the Yunnan government's order to close down a coal mine?" Mr. Li asked at an urgent meeting convened by the government agency. "What kind of behaviour is this? I was told there was not only one illegal coal mine in Qujing city, but 23 of them. This is a completely grotesque tale."

DIFFERENTIATION:

In preparing to write

the short stories,

pair students

who have strong writing skills

with other students

who may be

more creative

but need help

in writing their stories.

Authorities focused today on placating relatives of 181 men trapped underground in a flooded coal mine with little hope of rescue after a clash between managers and anguished families demanding information. The miners have been trapped since Friday when a dyke burst in torrential rains, sending water rushing into the mine shafts in the eastern province of Shandong. "For those family members of miners who rushed to the site, the local government is actively working to settle them in accommodation and has brought people to greet and console them in order to safeguard order and stability in the coal mining area," said a notice on the central government's website. As hopes faded for the miners, relatives were disputing the government's view of the flood as a natural disaster as their anger mounted. "The weather is a factor, but man-made factors are also extremely large. Last year, there was also a leak in the mine, so I wouldn't want the government to jump to a conclusion about the cause," said Zhang Chunling, whose brother is one of the missing.

Well, the standard procedure if you have time to gather up the materials and do it is to get cinder blocks or stoppings and you find a suitable spot and you build a wall and plaster it air tight. Then you grab what's available, a curtain or anything, and you curtain off what you can and you try to seal it. If you can't find anything else, you use mud from the bottom. You're talking about desperate times there. I'm sorry. I was just —. Explaining that part of it. I was close to all them guys that got killed and I know what they went through. Men that got killed. That was my crew.

CODA

MORGANTOWN, W.Va., Sept 27 (AP) – Two miners whose jobs included watching for safety hazards inside the Sago Mine before the deadly explosion last January committed suicide in the past month. Neither man had been blamed for the disaster that killed 12 of their comrades, and neither one's family has definitively linked the suicides to the accident. Both men were working at the Sago Mine on the day of the blast and were questioned by investigators along with dozens of other witnesses. One former co-worker said at least one of the men felt investigators were treating him as if he had done something wrong. John N. Boni, whose job that day was to maintain water pumps, shot himself Saturday at his home in Volga, the state police said. William L. Chisolm, 47, the dispatcher responsible for monitoring carbon monoxide alarms and communicating with crews underground that morning, shot himself at his Belington home on Aug. 29, the authorities said. State and federal mine-safety agencies have not determined the cause of the mine blast. But spokeswomen for both agencies said that both men had been thoroughly interviewed and that there had been no plans to talk with them again. International Coal Group, the mine's owner, has said it believes a lightning bolt somehow ignited methane gas that had accumulated naturally in a sealed-off section of the mine. Mr. Boni was certified as a fire boss and occasionally conducted preshift inspections to ensure the safety of incoming crews. Mr. Chisolm told investigators that a carbon monoxide alarm had sounded about 20 minutes before the explosion. Following procedure, he alerted a crew inside the mine and asked it to verify the alarm because the system had a history of malfunctions. Relatives told investigators that Mr. Chisolm had been depressed about personal matters and drinking heavily in the weeks before his death. Friends and family said Mr. Boni retired shortly after the accident. His former wife, Vicki Boni, said he had never discussed the accident with her, but said, "I'm sure it had weighed on his mind." Ms. Boni, who divorced Mr. Boni 15 years ago but saw him when he picked up their daughter for visits, said her own father died in a coal mine accident when she was a teenager. "It's something you never get over," she said.

WORKS CITED

Quotes from the three lessons are excerpted from the American Coal Foundation's "Lesson Plans" <http://www.teachcoal.org/lessonplans/index.html>. The American Coal Foundation (ACF) "was created in 1981 as a 501(c)(3) organization to develop, produce and disseminate, via the web, coal-related educational materials and programs designed for teachers and students. The ACF does not engage in lobbying."

Boldface quotes are verbatim excerpts from over 6,300 pages of testimony transcripts housed at the West Virginia Office of Miners' Health and Safety website, <http://www.wvminesafety.org/sagointerviews.htm>. These testimonies were recorded between January 17, 2006 and June 19, 2006.

Italicized quotations, in the order they appear in the text, are from the following sources:

Shi, Ting. "The day that all miners' wives dread." *South China Morning Post.* February 16, 2005: 4.

Dickie, Mure. "World's riskiest mines claim 200 lives." *Financial Times.* February 16, 2005: 10.

Ma, Josephine. "Family living in hell waiting for news." *South China Morning Post.* February 17, 2005: 5.

Reuters in Fuxin with Shi Ting. "First victims cremated under tight security." *South China Morning Post.* February 19, 2005: 5.

"NE China colliery beneath-shaft rescue work ends." *Xinhua News Agency.* February 22, 2005: 1.

Cui, Vivien. "Death toll from gas blast at coal mines reaches 60." *South China Morning Post.* March 21, 2005: 4.

Shi, Ting. "Women fear for spouses lost in blast." *South China Morning Post.* April 7, 2005: 6.

"Death toll in NW China coal mine explosion rises to 21." *Xinhua News Agency.* May 3, 2005: 1.

Guo, Nei. "Rescuers in bid to save 51 trapped miners." *China Daily.* May 20, 2005: 1.

"Death toll rises to 45 in north China coal mine blast." *Xinhua News Agency.* May 23, 2005: 1.

Fu, Jing. "Coal mine tragedies leave endless suffering." *China Daily.* May 26, 2005: 5.

Shirley Wu and Agencies in Beijing. "Mine owners hid 17 bodies after blast." *South China Morning Post.* July 15, 2005: 7.

Wu, Shirley. "Mine operators condemned for putting profits ahead of safety." *South China Morning Post.* July 16, 2005: 6.

Ma, Lie. "Mine blast death toll reaches 26." *China Daily.* July 22, 2005: 3.

Chan, Minnie. "Mayors suspended after mine floods." *South China Morning Post.* August 11, 2005: 6.

Magnier, Mark. "Hope fades for 122 trapped coal miners in China." *Chicago Tribune.* August 16, 2005: 5.

"123 trapped pitmen considered dead as subsidence forces end to recovery effort." *South China Morning Post.* August 30, 2005: 6.

Ma, Lie. "Authorities investigate coal mine cover-ups." *China Daily.* September 20, 2005: 3.

Chan, Minnie. "Five die in explosion at Xinjiang coal mine." *South China Morning Post.* October 5, 2005: 4.

McDonald, Joe. "China reports 138 dead after coal mine blast." *Chicago Tribune.* November 29, 2005: 6.

Yu, Verna. "Coal mine blast kills 134 in China." *National Post.* November 29, 2005: A15.

Fu, Jing. "Miners see no light at the end of the tunnel." *China Daily.* November 30, 2005: 5.

Ang, Audra. "Score killed in China mine blast." *Journal – Gazette.* December 8, 2005: 9A.

Cai, Jane. "Death toll rises to 74 at latest pit of misery." *South China Morning Post.* December 9, 2005: 7.

Jiang, Zhuqing. "After the smoke clears . . ." *China Daily.* December 10, 2005: 3.

Harmsen, Peter. "Outcry follows week of Chinese mine accidents." *National Post.* December 10, 2005: A19.

Xiao, Liu. "Gas blast in Shanxi mine kills at least 23." *China Daily.* February 3, 2006: 1.

Fu, Jing. "Six killed, 12 missing in coal mine gas surge." *China Daily.* February 27, 2006: 3.

Jiang, Zhuqing. "37 killed in 3 coal mine blasts." *China Daily.* March 14, 2006: 1.

Jiang, Xuezhou. "Coal mine explosion kills 4 women." *China Daily.* April 11, 2006: 2.

Bodeen, Christopher. "Electric outages delay rescue of 57 trapped Chinese miners." *Journal – Gazette.* May 23, 2006: 7A.

Bodeen, Christopher. "Hope gone for 57 miners in China." *Charleston Daily Mail.* May 23, 2006: 3A.

Barboza, David. "A Chinese Village is Rocked by the Coal Industry." *New York Times.* June 23, 2006: C1.

"53 confirmed dead in north China colliery blast." *Xinhua News Agency.* July 19, 2006: 1.

"Coal mine collapse kills 13 in China's Xinjiang." *Xinhua News Agency.* August 14, 2006: 1.

Xie, Chuanjiao. "Gansu mine blast kills 29, 19 injured." *China Daily.* November 1, 2006: 2.

"Three days of colliery disasters leave 85 Chinese workers dead." *Xinhua News Agency.* November 27, 2006: 1.

Lee, Georgiana and Associated Press in Beijing. "Local cadres attacked over gas blast." *South China Morning Post.* November 29, 2006: 6.

Zhu, Charlie. "China turns to consoling miners' families." *Toronto Star.* August 21, 2007: AA1.

"2 at Sago Mine on Day of Blast Commit Suicide." *New York Times.* September 28, 2006: A21.

A poet and labor activist heralded by Adrienne Rich for "regenerating the rich tradition of working-class literature," **MARK NOWAK** regularly leads transnational poetry workshops between American and international trade unions. He is the author of *Revenants* and *Shut Up Shut Down,* a *New York Times Book Review* Editor's Choice and finalist for the Academy of American Poets' James Laughlin Award. A native of Buffalo, New York, he now lives in St. Paul, Minnesota.

A British photographer, **IAN TEH** has been documenting working conditions in China for over a decade. His photographs have appeared in publications such as *Newsweek, Time, The New Yorker,* and the UK *Independent Magazine* and have been widely exhibited. He has received numerous honors, including the World Press Master Class. He was a finalist for the CCF Foundation for Photography prize in 2004 and his work was recently acquired by the Los Angeles County Museum of Art. Presently he lives and works in London.

COLOPHON

Cold Mountain Elementary was designed at Coffee House Press,
in the historic Grain Belt Brewery's Bottling House near downtown Minneapolis.
The text is set in Garamond.

FUNDER ACKNOWLEDGMENTS

Coffee House Press is an independent nonprofit literary publisher. Our books are made possible through the generous support of grants and gifts from many foundations, corporate giving programs, state and federal support, and through donations from individuals who believe in the transformational power of literature. Coffee House receives major general operating support from the McKnight Foundation, the Bush Foundation, from Target, and from the Minnesota State Arts Board, through an appropriation by the Minnesota State Legislature and from the National Endowment for the Arts, a federal agency. Coffee House also receives support from: an anonymous donor; the Elmer L. and Eleanor J. Andersen Foundation; Bill Berkson; the James L. and Nancy J. Bildner Foundation; the Patrick and Aimee Butler Family Foundation; the Buuck Family Foundation; the law firm of Fredrikson & Byron, PA.; Jennifer Haugh; Anselm Hollo and Jane Dalrymple-Hollo; Jeffrey Hom; Stephen and Isabel Keating; the Kenneth Koch Literary Estate; Seymour Kornblum and Gerry Lauter; the Lenfestey Family Foundation; Ethan J. Litman; Mary McDermid; Rebecca Rand; the law firm of Schwegman, Lundberg, Woessner, PA.; Charles Steffey and Suzannah Martin; Jeffrey Sugerman; the James R. Thorpe Foundation; Stu Wilson and Mel Barker; the Archie D. & Bertha H. Walker Foundation; the Woessner Freeman Family Foundation; the Wood-Rill Foundation; and many other generous individual donors.

This activity is made possible in part by a grant from the Minnesota State Arts Board, through an appropriation by the Minnesota State Legislature and a grant from the National Endowment for the Arts. MINNESOTA STATE ARTS BOARD   TARGET.

To you and our many readers across the country,
we send our thanks for your continuing support.

Good books are brewing at coffeehousepress.org